NATIONAL GEOGRAPHIC KiDS

LOOK & LEARN

Colors!

SCHOLASTIC INC.

ORANGE

butterfly

pepper

balloon

pumpkin

socks

This is candy for a special after-dinner treat. Can you find everything orange?

GUESS WHAT?

It takes 7 to 21 days to make a jelly bean.

BLUE

shoes

blueberries

frog

blocks
cup
flower

Go to the fair to ride the Ferris wheel! Can you find everything blue?

GUESS WHAT?

The tallest Ferris wheel in the world is taller than 40 elephants stacked up high.

YELLOW

ruler

popsicle

flower

bananas

toy duck

school bus

This is a coral reef where lots of fish live. Can you find everything yellow?

GUESS WHAT?

There are more than 7,000 coral reefs in the world!

GREEN

bird

apple

leaf

beetle

crayon

broccoli

These are fruits and vegetables that make a healthy snack.

Can you find everything green?

GUESS WHAT?

The fruits and vegetables that you eat are all plants.

RED

ball

ladybug

sea star

cherries

bucket

flower

Come play in the ball pit!
Can you find everything red?

GUESS WHAT?

The biggest ball pit ever had more than 130,000 balls in it!

Colors are all around!

orange
butterfly

white
ice cream

blue
frog

purple
present

green
apple

brown
dog

yellow
bananas

pink
hat

red
flower

black
cat

What colors have you learned?

10 9 8 7 6 5 4 3 2 1 18 19 20 21 22/0

Printed in the U.S.A. 40

C=Corbis; GI=Getty Images; iS=iStockphoto.com; JI=Jupiter Images; SS=Shutterstock
Cover, Frank and Helena Herholdt/JI; 2 (low left), Ingram; 2 (top), SvetlanaLarina/SS; 2-3 (low right), Ana de Sousa/SS; 3 (top), J. Helgason/SS; 3(low), tatniz/SS; 4-5, Cheryl E. Davis/SS; 6 (top L), Aaron Amat/SS; 6 (top R), Lepas/SS; 6 (low), Eric Isselée/SS; 7 (top), Loskutnikov/SS; 7 (lowL), Albo003/SS; 7 (low R), jeka84/SS; 8-9, buchan/SS; 10 (low L),Madlen/SS; 10 (top L), Kuzmin Andrey/SS; 10 (low R), mikeledray/SS;10 (top R), Nattika/SS; 11 (top), PhotoDisc; 11 (low), Rich Koele/SS; 12-13, Georgette Douwma/GI; 13 (low), Royalty-Free/C; 14 (low L), atoss/SS; 14 (top), Marina Jay/SS; 14 (low R), mvp23/SS; 15 (top L), BrookeBecker/SS; 15 (top R), irin-k/SS; 15 (low R), Reika/SS; 16-17, Bogda-nWankowicz/SS; 18 (top), Lawrence Manning/C; 18 (low), Elena Schweitzer/SS; 18 (R), Alexandr Pakhnyushchyy/iS; 19 (top L), Alex Staroseltsev/SS; 19(top R), Quayside/SS; 19 (low), Brand X; 20-21, Michele Galli/iS; 22 (A),Svetlana Larina/SS; 22 (B), Eric Isselée/SS; 22 (C), atoss/SS; 22 (D), Nattika/SS; 22 (E), Brand X; 22 (F), Elena Elisseeva/SS; 22 (G), Ragnarock/SS; 22 (H), Jagodka/SS; 22 (I), Vaclav Volrab/SS; 22 (J), Pixel Memoirs/SS; 23, Flickr RF/GI